THE
SPIRIT-FILLED
POCKET BIBLE
ON
HEALING

THE
SPIRIT-FILLED
POCKET BIBLE
ON
HEALING

HARRISON HOUSE, INC.
Tulsa, Oklahoma

The Spirit-Filled Pocket Bible on Healing
ISBN 0-89274-832-X
Copyright © 1995 by Harrison House, Inc.
P. O. Box 35035
Tulsa, OK 74153

Published by Harrison House, Inc.
P. O. Box 35035
Tulsa, OK 74153

The
Spirit-Filled
Pocket Bible
on Healing

Presented to

_____

By

_____

Date

_____

*I*ntroduction

First Peter 2:24 in the *Moffatt Translation* of the Bible says, His [Jesus'] bruising *was* your healing. Past tense! *The Amplified Bible* of this verse says, By His wounds you *have been* healed. Again, past tense!

If the bruising and wounds Jesus took at Calvary were for our healing — as well as for our righteousness and prosperity — why are so many Christians sick in their minds and bodies?

Solomon said God's Word is *life* and *health* to the person who will meditate upon it and not let it depart from his or her eyes or heart. (Proverbs 4:20-22.)

It's time to rise up in your faith — believing and speaking what God says, as opposed to what circumstances dictate — for the resurrection Spirit that is alive in you as a child of God and that is alive in God's Word is greater than any sickness or disease. The compilation of healing Scriptures in this Pocket Bible has been made to help you rise up in your inner man and throw off all of the oppressive works of the devil (Acts 10:38) by believing, receiving, confessing and acting upon these healing truths.

*P*rayer

Father, I now understand that it is Your will that I walk in completeness, soundness and perfect wholeness in my spirit, soul and body. Jesus Christ, Your Son, and now my Lord and Savior, paid the price in full at Calvary's cross for my health and well-being. I refuse to be robbed of this provision any longer, in Jesus' name.

The alien forces of wrong thoughts, oppression, depression, torment, fear, affliction, infirmity, sickness and disease cannot reside in me, because You live in me now, Lord Jesus, through the Person of the Holy Spirit. With the authority You have invested in me I command every alien force to be replaced by Your resurrection power.

Today, I receive an exchange of Your strength for my weakness; Your joy for my sadness; Your pleasure and delight for my sorrow and heaviness; Your hope for my despair; Your peace for my torment; Your prosperity of spirit, body, mind, finances and relationships for any lack I have experienced; Your ability for my inability; Your acceptance for my rejection; Your obedience for my rebellion; Your encouragement for my discouragement; Your soundness for my brokenness; Your comfort for my pain; and Your courage, Lord, for my fear and timidity.

I command my muscles, tissues, cells and blood to come in line now with Your resurrection life, Lord Jesus. Thank You for fully aligning my spirit, body and mind — and every other area of my life — with Your perfect soundness provided for me through Your shed blood at Calvary, Lord Jesus. Through daily doses of Your Word and meditation upon Your promises, Lord, I will walk in divine health, in Jesus' name. Amen.

If thou wilt diligently hearken to the voice of the Lord thy God, and wilt do that which is right in his sight, and wilt give ear to his commandments, and keep all his statutes, I will put none of these diseases upon thee, which I have brought upon the Egyptians: *for I am the Lord that healeth thee.*

Exodus 15:26

I, the Lord, am your healer.

Exodus 15:26b NASB

Honour thy father and thy mother: that thy days may be long upon the land which the Lord thy God giveth thee.

Exodus 20:12

So you shall serve the Lord your God, and He will bless your bread and your water. And I will take sickness away from the midst of you.

No one shall suffer miscarriage or be barren in your land; I will fulfill the number of your days.

Exodus 23:25,26 NKJV

You shall serve the Lord your God only; then I will bless you with food and with water, and I will take away sickness from among you.

There will be no miscarriages nor barrenness throughout your land, and you will live out the full quota of the days of your life.

Exodus 23:25,26 TLB

God is not a man, that he should lie, nor a son of man, that he should change his mind. Does he speak and then not act? Does he promise and not fulfill?

Numbers 23:19 NIV

Thou shalt therefore keep the commandments, and the statutes, and the judgments, which I command thee this day, to do them.

Wherefore it shall come to pass, if ye hearken to these judgments, and keep, and do them, that the Lord thy God shall keep unto thee the covenant and the mercy which he sware unto thy fathers:

And he will love thee, and bless thee, and multiply thee: he will also bless the fruit of thy womb, and the fruit of thy land, thy corn, and thy wine, and thine oil, the increase of thy kine, and the flocks of thy sheep, in the land which he sware unto thy fathers to give thee.

Thou shalt be blessed above all people: there shall not be male or female barren among you, or among your cattle.

And the Lord will take away from thee all sickness, and will put none of the evil diseases of Egypt, which thou knowest, upon thee; but will lay them upon all them that hate thee.

Deuteronomy 7:11-15

If you fully obey the Lord your God and carefully follow all his commands I give you today, the Lord your God will set you high above all the nations on earth. All these blessings will come upon you and accompany you if you obey the Lord your God:

You will be blessed in the city and blessed in the country.

The fruit of your womb will be blessed, and the crops of your land and the young of your livestock — the calves of your herds and the lambs of your flocks.

Your basket and your kneading trough will be blessed.

You will be blessed when you come in and blessed when you go out.

The Lord will grant that the enemies who rise up against you will be defeated before you. They will come at you from one direction but flee from you in seven.

The Lord will send a blessing on your barns and on everything you put your hand to. The Lord your God will bless you in the land he is giving you.

The Lord will establish you as his holy people, as he promised you on oath, if you keep the commands of the Lord your God and walk in his ways. Then all the peoples on earth will see that you are called by the name of the Lord, and they will fear you.

The Lord will grant you abundant prosperity — in the fruit of your womb, the young of your livestock and the crops of your ground — in the land he swore to your forefathers to give you.

The Lord will open the heavens, the storehouse of his bounty, to send rain on your land in season and to bless all the work of your hands. You will lend to many nations but will borrow from none. The Lord will make you the head, not the tail. If you pay attention to the commands of the Lord your God that I give you this day and carefully follow them, you will always be at the top, never at the bottom.

Deuteronomy 28:1-13 NIV

I call heaven and earth to witness this day against you that I have set before you life and death, the blessings and the curses; therefore choose life, that you and your descendants may live

And may love the Lord your God, obey His voice, and cling to Him. For He is your life and the length of your days.

Deuteronomy 30:19,20a AMP

Now Naaman, commander of the army of the king of Syria, was a great and honorable man in the eyes of his master, because by him the Lord had given victory to Syria. He was also a mighty man of valor, but a leper.

And the Syrians had gone out on raids, and had brought back captive a young girl from the land of Israel. She waited on Naaman's wife.

Then she said to her mistress, "If only my master were with the prophet who is in Samaria! For he would heal him of his leprosy."

And Naaman went in and told his master, saying, "Thus and thus said the girl who is from the land of Israel."

Then the king of Syria said, "Go now, and I will send a letter to the king of Israel." So he departed and took with him ten talents of silver, six thousand shekels of gold, and ten changes of clothing.

Then he brought the letter to the king of Israel, which said,

> Now be advised, when this letter comes to you, that I have sent Naaman my servant to you, that you may heal him of his leprosy.

And it happened, when the king of Israel read the letter, that he tore his clothes and said, "Am I God, to kill and make alive, that this man sends a man to me to heal him of his leprosy? Therefore please consider, and see how he seeks a quarrel with me."

So it was, when Elisha the man of God heard that the king of Israel had torn his clothes, that he sent to the king, saying, "Why have you torn your clothes? Please let him come to me, and he shall know that there is a prophet in Israel."

Then Naaman went with his horses and chariot, and he stood at the door of Elisha's house.

And Elisha sent a messenger to him, saying, "Go and wash in the Jordan seven times, and your flesh shall be restored to you, and you shall be clean."

But Naaman became furious, and went away and said, "Indeed, I said to myself, 'He will surely come out to me, and stand and call on the name of the Lord his God, and wave his hand over the place, and heal the leprosy.'

"Are not the Abanah and the Pharpar, the rivers of Damascus, better than all the waters of Israel? Could I not wash in them and be clean?" So he turned and went away in a rage.

And his servants came near and spoke to him, and said, "My father, if the prophet had told you to do something great, would you not have done it? How much more then, when he says to you, 'Wash, and be clean'?"

So he went down and dipped seven times in the Jordan, according to the saying of the man of God; and his flesh was restored like the flesh of a little child, and he was clean.

2 Kings 5:1-14 NKJV

For the joy of the Lord is your strength.

Nehemiah 8:10b

Have pity on me, Eternal, in my weakness, oh heal me, for my health is broken.

Psalm 6:2
Moffatt's Trans.

He asked for a long, good life, and you have granted his request; the days of his life stretch on and on forever.

Psalm 21:4 TLB

O Lord my God, I called to you for help and you healed me.

Psalm 30:2 NIV

Be of good courage, and he shall strength-

en your heart, all ye that hope in the Lord.
Psalm 31:24

Do you want a long, good life?

Then watch your tongue! Keep your
lips from lying.
Psalm 34:12,13 TLB

What man is he who desires life and longs
for many days, that he may see good?

Keep your tongue from evil and your
lips from speaking deceit.
Psalm 34:12,13 AMP

When the righteous cry for help, the Lord
hears, and delivers them out of *all* their
distress and troubles.

The Lord is close to those who are of a
broken heart and saves such as are crushed
with sorrow for sin and are humbly and
thoroughly penitent.
Psalm 34:17,18 AMP

Many evils confront the [consistently]
righteous, but the Lord delivers him out of
them all.

19

He keeps all his bones; not one of them is broken.

Psalm 34:19,20 AMP

The Lord will sustain him on his sickbed and restore him from his bed of illness.

I said, "O Lord, have mercy on me; heal me, for I have sinned against you."

Psalm 41:3,4 NIV

God be merciful unto us, and bless us; and cause his face to shine upon us; Selah.

That thy way may be known upon earth, thy saving health among all nations.

Psalm 67:1,2

Blessed be the Lord, who daily loadeth us with benefits.

Psalm 68:19a

The days of our years are threescore years and ten; and if by reason of strength they be fourscore years.

Psalm 90:10a

He who dwells in the secret place of the

Most High shall abide under the shadow of the Almighty.

I will say of the Lord, "He is my refuge and my fortress; My God, in Him I will trust."

Surely He shall deliver you from the snare of the fowler and from the perilous pestilence.

Psalm 91:1-3 NKJV

No evil shall befall you, nor shall any plague come near your dwelling;

For He shall give His angels charge over you, to keep you in all your ways.

In their hands they shall bear you up, lest you dash your foot against a stone.

You shall tread upon the lion and the cobra, the young lion and the serpent you shall trample underfoot.

"Because he has set his love upon Me, therefore I will deliver him; I will set him on high, because he has known My name.

"He shall call upon Me, and I will answer him; I will be with him in trouble; I will deliver him and honor him.

"With long life I will satisfy him, and show him My salvation."

Psalm 91:10-16 NKJV

The [uncompromisingly] righteous shall flourish like the palm tree [be long-lived, stately, upright, useful, and fruitful]; they shall grow like a cedar in Lebanon [majestic, stable, durable, and incorruptible].

Planted in the house of the Lord, they shall flourish in the courts of our God.

[Growing in grace] they shall still bring forth fruit in old age; they shall be full of sap [of spiritual vitality] and [rich in the] verdure [of trust, love, and contentment];

[They are living memorials] to show that the Lord is upright and faithful to His promises; He is my Rock, and there is no unrighteousness in Him.

Psalm 92:12-15 AMP

Bless the Lord, O my soul, and forget not all his benefits:

Who forgiveth all thine iniquities; who healeth all thy diseases;

Who redeemeth thy life from destruction; who crowneth thee with lovingkindness and tender mercies;

Who satisfieth thy mouth with good

things; so that thy youth is renewed like the eagle's.

Psalm 103:2-5

He brought them forth also with silver and gold: and there was not one feeble person among their tribes.

Psalm 105:37

He sent his word, and healed them, and delivered them from their destructions.

Psalm 107:20

He maketh the barren woman to keep house, and to be a joyful mother of children.

Psalm 113:9

I shall not die, but live, and declare the works of the Lord.

Psalm 118:17

I will lift up mine eyes unto the hills, from whence cometh my help.

My help cometh from the Lord, which made heaven and earth.

23

He will not suffer thy foot to be moved: he that keepeth thee will not slumber.

Behold, he that keepeth Israel shall neither slumber nor sleep.

The Lord is thy keeper: the Lord is thy shade upon thy right hand.

The sun shall not smite thee by day, nor the moon by night.

The Lord shall preserve thee from *all* evil: he shall preserve thy soul.

The Lord shall preserve thy going out and thy coming in from this time forth, and even for evermore.

Psalm 121:1-8

It is vain for you to rise up early, to sit up late, to eat the bread of sorrows: for so he giveth his beloved sleep.

Psalm 127:2

The Lord will perfect that which concerns me.

Psalm 138:8a AMP

He heals the brokenhearted and binds up

their wounds [curing their pains and their sorrows].

Psalm 147:3 AMP

My son, forget not my law; but let thine heart keep my commandments;

For length of days, and long life, and peace, shall they add to thee.

Proverbs 3:1,2

Do not be wise in your own eyes; fear the Lord and depart from evil.

It will be health to your flesh, and strength to your bones.

Proverbs 3:7,8 NKJV

Never pride yourself on your own wisdom, revere the Eternal and draw back from sin:

That will mean health for your body and fresh life to your frame.

Proverbs 3:7,8
Moffatt's Trans.

Length of days is in her [wisdom's] right

hand; and in her left hand riches and honour.

Proverbs 3:16

My son, attend to my words; incline thine ear unto my sayings.

Let them not depart from thine eyes; keep them in the midst of thine heart.

For they are life unto those that find them, and health to all their flesh.

Proverbs 4:20-22

Keep my commandments, and live; and my law as the apple of thine eye.

Proverbs 7:2

For by me [wisdom] thy days shall be multiplied, and the years of thy life shall be increased.

Proverbs 9:11

The mouth of a righteous man is a well of life.

Proverbs 10:11a

The talk of good men is a life-giving fountain.

> *Proverbs 10:11a*
> *Moffatt's Trans.*

The reverent and worshipful fear of the Lord prolongs one's days, but the years of the wicked shall be made short.

> *Proverbs 10:27* AMP

As righteousness tendeth to life: so he that pursueth evil pursueth it to his own death.

> *Proverbs 11:19*

Reckless words pierce like a sword, but the tongue of the wise brings healing.

> *Proverbs 12:18* NIV

In the way of righteousness is life; and in the pathway thereof there is no death.

> *Proverbs 12:28*

A sound heart is life to the body, but envy is rottenness to the bones.

> *Proverbs 14:30* NKJV

A calm and undisturbed mind and heart are the life and health of the body, but envy, jealousy, and wrath are like rottenness of the bones.

Proverbs 14:30 AMP

A wholesome tongue is a tree of life.

Proverbs 15:4a

A merry heart maketh a cheerful countenance: but by sorrow of the heart the spirit is broken.

Proverbs 15:13

A cheerful look brings joy to the heart, and good news gives health to the bones.

Proverbs 15:30 NIV

Pleasant words are as an honeycomb, sweet to the soul, and health to the bones.

Proverbs 16:24

Kind words are like honey — enjoyable and healthful.

Proverbs 16:24 TLB

A glad heart helps and heals: a broken spirit saps vitality.

Proverbs 17:22
Moffatt's Trans.

A happy heart is good medicine and a cheerful mind works healing, but a broken spirit dries up the bones.

Proverbs 17:22 AMP

A man's stomach shall be satisfied from the fruit of his mouth; from the produce of his lips he shall be filled.

Death and life are in the power of the tongue, and those who love it will eat its fruit.

Proverbs 18:20,21 NKJV

Thou wilt keep him in perfect peace, whose mind is stayed on thee: because he trusteth in thee.

Trust ye in the Lord for ever: for in the Lord JEHOVAH is everlasting strength.

Isaiah 26:3,4

For with stammering lips and another

29

tongue will he speak to this people.

To whom he said, This is the rest wherewith ye may cause the weary to rest; and this is the refreshing.

Isaiah 28:11,12

And the eyes of them that see shall not be dim, and the ears of them that hear shall hearken.

The heart also of the rash shall understand knowledge, and the tongue of the stammerers shall be ready to speak plainly.

Isaiah 32:3,4

Strengthen ye the weak hands, and confirm the feeble knees.

Isaiah 35:3

Then the eyes of the blind shall be opened, and the ears of the deaf shall be unstopped.

Isaiah 35:5

Then shall the lame man leap as an hart, and the tongue of the dumb sing.

Isaiah 35:6a

He gives strength to the weary and increases the power of the weak.

Even youths grow tired and weary, and young men stumble and fall;

But those who hope in the Lord will renew their strength. They will soar on wings like eagles; they will run and not grow weary, they will walk and not be faint.

Isaiah 40:29-31NIV

Hear, ye deaf; and look, ye blind, that ye may see.

Isaiah 42:18

But now, thus says the Lord, your Creator, O Jacob, and He who formed you, O Israel, "Do not fear, for I have redeemed you; I have called you by name; you are Mine!

"When you pass through the waters, I will be with you; and through the rivers, they will not overflow you. When you walk through the fire, you will not be scorched, nor will the flame burn you."

Isaiah 43:1,2 NASB

Surely He has borne our griefs and carried

our sorrows; yet we esteemed Him stricken, smitten by God, and afflicted.

But He was wounded for our transgressions, He was bruised for our iniquities; the chastisement for our peace was upon Him, and by His stripes we are healed.

Isaiah 53:4,5 NKJV

No weapon that is formed against thee shall prosper; and every tongue that shall rise against thee in judgment thou shalt condemn. This is the heritage of the servants of the Lord, and their righteousness is of me, saith the Lord.

Isaiah 54:17

So shall my word be that goeth forth out of my mouth: it shall not return unto me void, but it shall accomplish that which I please, and it shall prosper in the thing whereto I sent it.

Isaiah 55:11

I have seen his [willful] ways, but I will heal him; I will lead him also and will recompense him and restore comfort to him and to those who mourn for him.

Peace, peace, to him who is far off [both Jew and Gentile] and to him who is near! says the Lord; I create the fruit of his lips, and I will heal him [make his lips blossom anew with speech in thankful praise].

Isaiah 57:18,19 AMP

Then shall your light break forth like the morning, and your healing (your restoration and the power of a new life) shall spring forth speedily; your righteousness (your rightness, your justice, and your right relationship with God) shall go before you [conducting you to peace and prosperity], and the glory of the Lord shall be your rear guard.

Isaiah 58:8 AMP

And the Lord shall guide thee continually, and satisfy thy soul in drought, and make fat thy bones: and thou shalt be like a watered garden, and like a spring of water, whose waters fail not.

Isaiah 58:11

They shall not build, and another inhabit; they shall not plant, and another eat: for as the days of a tree are the days of my people, and mine elect shall long enjoy the work of their hands.

They shall not labour in vain, nor bring forth for trouble; for they are the seed of the blessed of the Lord, and their offspring with them.

And it shall come to pass, that before they call, I will answer; and while they are yet speaking, I will hear.

Isaiah 65:22-24

For I will hasten my word to perform it.

Jeremiah 1:12b

Turn back, you turncoat [rebellious] children, and I will heal your hurt.

Jeremiah 3:22
Moffatt's Trans.

Heal me, O Lord, and I shall be healed; save me, and I shall be saved: for thou art my praise.

Jeremiah 17:14

"For I know the plans I have for you," declares the Lord, "plans to prosper you and not to harm you, plans to give you hope and a future."

Jeremiah 29:11 NIV

"For I will restore you to health and I will heal you of your wounds," declares the Lord.

Jeremiah 30:17a NASB

Nevertheless, I will bring health and healing to it; I will heal my people and will let them enjoy abundant peace and security.

Jeremiah 33:6 NIV

And when I passed by thee, and saw thee polluted in thine own blood, I said unto thee when thou wast in thy blood, Live; yea, I said unto thee when thou wast in thy blood, Live.

Ezekiel 16:6

I will heal their backsliding, I will love them freely: for mine anger is turned away from him.

Hosea 14:4

Let the weak say, I am strong.
Joel 3:10b

For I am the Lord, I change not.
Malachi 3:6a

But unto you who revere and worshipful-ly fear My name shall the Sun of Righteousness arise with healing in His wings and His beams, and you shall go forth and gambol like calves [released] from the stall and leap for joy.

And you shall tread down the lawless and wicked, for they shall be ashes under the soles of your feet in the day that I shall do this, says the Lord of hosts.
Malachi 4:2,3 AMP

And Jesus went about all Galilee, teaching in their synagogues, preaching the gospel of the kingdom, and *healing* all kinds of sickness and all kinds of disease among the people.

Then His fame went throughout all Syria; and they brought to Him all sick people who were afflicted with various diseases and torments, and those who were demon-possessed, epileptics, and paralytics; and He healed them.

Matthew 4:23,24 NKJV

And, behold, there came a leper and worshipped him, saying, Lord, if thou wilt, thou canst make me clean.

And Jesus put forth his hand, and touched him, saying, I will; be thou clean. And immediately his leprosy was cleansed.

Matthew 8:2,3

And when Jesus was entered into Capernaum, there came unto him a centurion, beseeching him,

And saying, Lord, my servant lieth at home sick of the palsy, grievously tormented.

And Jesus saith unto him, I will come and heal him.

The centurion answered and said, Lord, I am not worthy that thou shouldest come under my roof: but speak the word only, and my servant shall be healed.

For I am a man under authority, having soldiers under me: and I say to this man, Go, and he goeth; and to another, Come, and he cometh; and to my servant, Do this, and he doeth it.

When Jesus heard it, he marvelled, and said to them that followed, Verily I say unto you, I have not found so great faith, no, not in Israel...

And Jesus said unto the centurion, Go thy way; and as thou hast believed, so be it done unto thee. And his servant was healed in the selfsame hour.

Matthew 8:5-10,13

And when Jesus was come into Peter's house, he saw his wife's mother laid, and sick of a fever.

And he touched her hand, and the fever left her: and she arose, and ministered unto them.

Matthew 8:14,15

When evening had come, they brought to Him many who were demon-possessed. And He cast out the spirits with a word, and healed all who were sick,

That it might be fulfilled which was spoken by Isaiah the prophet, saying: "He

Himself took our infirmities and bore our sicknesses."

Matthew 8:16,17 NKJV

In the evening the people brought to Jesus many who were possessed by demons; and he drove out the spirits with a word, and cured all who were ill, in fulfilment of these words in the Prophet Isaiah — "He took our infirmities on himself, and bore the burden of our diseases."

Matthew 8:16,17
The Twentieth Century
New Testament

And, behold, they brought to him a man sick of the palsy, lying on a bed: and Jesus seeing their faith said unto the sick of the palsy; Son, be of good cheer; thy sins be forgiven thee.

And he arose, and departed to his house.

Matthew 9:2,7

While he spake these things unto them, behold, there came a certain ruler, and worshipped him, saying, My daughter is even now dead: but come and lay thy hand upon her, and she shall live.

And Jesus arose, and followed him, and so did his disciples.

And when Jesus came into the ruler's house, and saw the minstrels and the people making a noise,

He said unto them. Give place: for the maid is not dead, but sleepeth. And they laughed him to scorn.

But when the people were put forth, he went in, and took her by the hand, and the maid arose.

Matthew 9:18,19,23-25

And when Jesus departed thence, two blind men followed him, crying, and saying, Thou Son of David, have mercy on us.

And when he was come into the house, the blind men came to him: and Jesus saith unto them, Believe ye that I am able to do this? They said unto him, Yea, Lord.

Then touched he their eyes, saying, According to your faith be it unto you.

And their eyes were opened; and Jesus straitly charged them, saying, See that no man know it.

But they, when they were departed, spread abroad his fame in all that country.

Matthew 9:27-31

As they went out, behold, they brought to him a dumb man possessed with a devil.

And when the devil was cast out, the dumb spake.

Matthew 9:32,33a

And Jesus went about all the cities and villages, teaching in their synagogues, and preaching the gospel of the kingdom, and healing every sickness and every disease among the people.

Matthew 9:35

And when He had called His twelve disciples to Him, He gave them power over unclean spirits, to cast them out, and to heal all kinds of sickness and all kinds of disease...

"And as you go, preach, saying, 'The kingdom of heaven is at hand.'"

"Heal the sick, cleanse the lepers, raise

the dead, cast out demons. Freely you have received, freely give.

Matthew 10:1,7,8 NKJV

Now when John had heard in the prison the works of Christ, he sent two of his disciples,

And said unto him, Art thou he that should come, or do we look for another?

Jesus answered and said unto them, Go and shew John again those things which ye do hear and see:

The blind receive their sight, and the lame walk, the lepers are cleansed, and the deaf hear, the dead are raised up, and the poor have the gospel preached to them.

Matthew 11:2-5

Come to me, all who are growing weary to the point of exhaustion, and who have been loaded with burdens and are bending beneath their weight, and I alone will cause you to cease from your labor and take away your burdens and thus refresh you with rest. Take at once my yoke upon you and learn from me, because I am meek and lowly in heart, and you will find cessation from labor and refreshment for your souls, for my yoke is mild and pleasant, and my load is light in weight.

Matthew 11:28-30

The Wuest New Testament

He went into their synagogue:

And, behold, there was a man which had his hand withered. And they asked him, saying, Is it lawful to heal on the sabbath days? that they might accuse him.

And he said unto them, What man shall there be among you, that shall have one sheep, and if it fall into a pit on the sabbath day, will he not lay hold on it, and lift it out?

How much then is a man better than a sheep? Wherefore it is lawful to do well on the sabbath days.

Then saith he to the man, Stretch forth thine hand. And he stretched it forth; and it was restored whole, like as the other.

Matthew 12:9-13

A number of people followed him [Jesus], and he cured them all.

Matthew 12:15b

The Twentieth Century
New Testament

Then was brought unto him one possessed with a devil, blind, and dumb: and he healed him, insomuch that the blind and dumb both spake and saw.

Matthew 12:22

When Jesus heard of it [of John the Baptist's beheading], he departed thence by ship into a desert place apart: and when the people had heard thereof, they followed him on foot out of the cities.

And Jesus went forth, and saw a great multitude, and was moved with compassion toward them, and he healed their sick.

Matthew 14:13,14

When they had crossed over, they came to the land of Gennesaret.

And when the men of that place recognized Him, they sent out into all that surrounding region, brought to Him all who were sick,

And begged Him that they might only touch the hem of His garment. And as many as touched it were made perfectly well.

Matthew 14:34-36 NKJV

And, behold, a woman of Canaan came out of the same coasts, and cried unto him, saying, Have mercy on me, O Lord, thou son of David; my daughter is grievously vexed with a devil.

But he answered her not a word. And his disciples came and besought him, saying, Send her away; for she crieth after us.

But he answered and said, I am not sent but unto the lost sheep of the house of Israel.

Then came she and worshipped him, saying, Lord, help me.

But he answered and said, It is not meet to take the children's bread, and to cast it to dogs.

And she said, Truth, Lord: yet the dogs eat of the crumbs which fall from their masters' table.

Then Jesus answered and said unto her, O woman, great is thy faith: be it unto thee even as thou wilt. And her daughter was made whole from that very hour.

Matthew 15:22-28

Then Jesus removed from that country and went along the sea of Galilee; he went up the hillside and sat there.

And large crowds came to him bringing the lame and the blind, the dumb, the maimed, and many others; they laid them at his feet, and he healed them.

This made the crowd wonder, to see dumb people speaking, the lame walking, and the blind seeing. And they glorified the God of Israel.

Matthew 15:29-31
Moffatt's Trans.

And when they had come to the multitude, a man came to Him, kneeling down to Him and saying,

"Lord, have mercy on my son, for he is an epileptic and suffers severely; for he often falls into the fire and often into the water.

"So I brought him to Your disciples, but they could not cure him."

Then Jesus answered and said, "O faithless and perverse generation, how long shall I be with you? How long shall I bear with you? Bring him here to Me."

And Jesus rebuked the demon, and it came out of him; and the child was cured from that very hour.

Then the disciples came to Jesus privately and said, "Why could we not cast it out?"

So Jesus said to them, "Because of your unbelief; for assuredly, I say to you, if you have faith as a mustard seed, you will say to this mountain, 'Move from here to there,' and it will move; and nothing will be impossible for you.

"However, this kind does not go out except by prayer and fasting."

Matthew 17:14-21 NKJV

Verily I say unto you, Whatsoever ye shall bind on earth shall be bound in heaven: and whatsoever ye shall loose on earth shall be loosed in heaven.

Again I say unto you, That if two of you shall agree on earth as touching any thing that they shall ask, it shall be done for them of my Father which is in heaven.

For where two or three are gathered together in my name, there am I in the midst of them.

Matthew 18:18-20

And it came to pass, that when Jesus had

finished these sayings, he departed from Galilee, and came into the coasts of Judaea beyond Jordan;

And great multitudes followed him; and he healed them there.

Matthew 19:1,2

And as they departed from Jericho, a great multitude followed him.

And, behold, two blind men sitting by the way side, when they heard that Jesus passed by, cried out, saying, Have mercy on us, O Lord, thou son of David.

And the multitude rebuked them, because they should hold their peace: but they cried the more, saying, Have mercy on us, O Lord, thou son of David.

And Jesus stood still, and called them, and said, What will ye that I shall do unto you?

They say unto him, Lord, that our eyes may be opened.

So Jesus had compassion on them, and touched their eyes: and immediately their eyes received sight, and they followed him.

Matthew 20:29-34

And the blind and the lame came to him in the temple; and he healed them.

Matthew 21:14

Now Simon's mother-in-law was lying sick with a fever; and immediately they spoke to Him [Jesus] about her.

And He came to her and raised her up, taking her by the hand, and the fever left her, and she waited on them.

Mark 1:30,31 NASB

And when evening had come, after the sun had set, they began bringing to Him all who were ill and those who were demon-possessed.

And the whole city had gathered at the door.

And He healed many who were ill with various diseases, and cast out many demons; and He was not permitting the demons to speak, because they knew who He was.

Mark 1:32-34 NASB

And again He entered Capernaum after

some days, and it was heard that He was in the house.

Immediately many gathered together, so that there was no longer room to receive them, not even near the door. And He preached the word to them.

Then they came to Him, bringing a paralytic who was carried by four men.

And when they could not come near Him because of the crowd, they uncovered the roof where He was. So when they had broken through, they let down the bed on which the paralytic was lying.

When Jesus saw their faith, He said to the paralytic, "Son, your sins are forgiven you."

And some of the scribes were sitting there and reasoning in their hearts,

"Why does this Man speak blasphemies like this? Who can forgive sins but God alone?"

But immediately, when Jesus perceived in His spirit that they reasoned thus within themselves, He said to them, "Why do you reason about these things in your hearts?

"Which is easier, to say to the paralytic, 'Your sins are forgiven you,' or to say, 'Arise, take up your bed and walk'?

"But that you may know that the Son of Man has power on earth to forgive sins" — He said to the paralytic,

"I say to you, arise, take up your bed, and go to your house."

Immediately he arose, took up the bed, and went out in the presence of them all, so that all were amazed and glorified God, saying, "We never saw anything like this!"

Mark 2:1-12 NKJV

He next entered the synagogue. Now a man was there whose hand was withered, and they watched to see if he would heal him on the sabbath, so as to get a charge against him. He said to the man with the withered hand, "Rise and come forward;" then he asked them, "Is it right to help or to hurt on the sabbath, to save life or to kill?" They were silent.

Then glancing round him in anger

and vexation at their obstinacy, he told the man, "Stretch out your hand." He stretched it out, and his hand was quite restored.

Mark 3:1-5

Moffatt's Trans.

And they came over unto the other side of the sea, into the country of the Gadarenes.

And when he was come out of the ship, immediately there met him out of the tombs a man with an unclean spirit,

Who had his dwelling among the tombs; and no man could bind him, no, not with chains:

Because that he had been often bound with fetters and chains, and the chains had been plucked asunder by him, and the fetters broken in pieces: neither could any man tame him.

And always, night and day, he was in the mountains, and in the tombs, crying, and cutting himself with stones.

But when he saw Jesus afar off, he ran and worshipped him,

And cried with a loud voice, and said, What have I to do with thee, Jesus, thou

Son of the most high God? I adjure thee by God, that thou torment me not.

For he said unto him, Come out of the man, thou unclean spirit.

And he asked him, What is thy name? And he answered, saying, My name is Legion: for we are many.

And he besought him much that he would not send them away out of the country.

Now there was there nigh unto the mountains a great herd of swine feeding.

And all the devils besought him, saying, Send us into the swine, that we may enter into them.

And forthwith Jesus gave them leave. And the unclean spirits went out, and entered into the swine: and the herd ran violently down a steep place into the sea, (they were about two thousand;) and were choked in the sea.

And they that fed the swine fled, and told it in the city, and in the country. And they went out to see what it was that was done.

And they come to Jesus, and see him that was possessed with the devil, and had the legion, sitting, and clothed, and in his right mind: and they were afraid.

And they that saw it told them how it befell to him that was possessed with the devil, and also concerning the swine.

And they began to pray him to depart out of their coasts.

And when he was come into the ship, he that had been possessed with the devil prayed him that he might be with him.

Howbeit Jesus suffered him not, but saith unto him, Go home to thy friends, and tell them how great things the Lord hath done for thee, and hath had compassion on thee.

And he departed, and began to publish in Decapolis how great things Jesus had done for him: and all men did marvel.

Mark 5:1-20

And when Jesus was passed over again by ship unto the other side, much people gathered unto him: and he was nigh unto the sea.

And, behold, there cometh one of the rulers of the synagogue, Jairus by name; and when he saw him, he fell at his feet,

And besought him greatly, saying, My little daughter lieth at the point of death: I pray thee, come and lay thy hands on her, that she may be healed; and she shall live.

And Jesus went with him; and much people followed him, and thronged him.

Mark 5:21-24

And a certain woman, which had an issue of blood twelve years,

And had suffered many things of many physicians, and had spent all that she had, and was nothing bettered, but rather grew worse,

When she had heard of Jesus, came in the press behind, and touched his garment.

For she said, If I may touch but his clothes, I shall be whole.

And straightway the fountain of her blood was dried up; and she felt in her body that she was healed of that plague.

And Jesus, immediately knowing in himself that virtue had gone out of him, turned him about in the press, and said, Who touched my clothes?

And his disciples said unto him, Thou seest the multitude thronging thee, and sayest thou, Who touched me?

And he looked round about to see her that had done this thing.

But the woman fearing and trembling, knowing what was done in her, came and fell down before him, and told him all the truth.

And he said unto her, Daughter, thy faith hath made thee whole; go in peace, and be whole of thy plague.

While he yet spake, there came from the ruler of the synagogue's house certain which said, Thy daughter is dead: why troublest thou the Master any further?

As soon as Jesus heard the word that was spoken, he saith unto the ruler of the synagogue, Be not afraid, only believe.

And he suffered no man to follow him, save Peter, and James, and John the brother of James.

And he cometh to the house of the ruler of the synagogue, and seeth the tumult, and them that wept and wailed greatly.

And when he was come in, he saith unto them, Why make ye this ado, and weep? the damsel is not dead, but sleepeth.

And they laughed him to scorn. But when he had put them all out, he taketh the father and the mother of the damsel, and them that were with him, and entered in where the damsel was lying.

And he took the damsel by the hand, and said unto her, Talitha cumi; which is, being interpreted, Damsel, I say unto thee, arise.

And straightway the damsel arose, and walked; for she was of the age of twelve years. And they were astonished with a great astonishment.

And he charged them straitly that no man should know it; and commanded that something should be given her to eat.

Mark 5:25-43

When they had crossed over, they landed at Gennesaret, and moored the boat.

But they had no sooner left her than the people, recognizing Jesus, hurried over the whole country-side, and began to carry about upon mats those who were ill, wherever they heard he was.

So wherever he went — to villages, or towns, or farms — they would lay their sick in the market-places, begging him to let them touch only the tassel of his cloak; and all who touched were made well.

Mark 6:53-56
The Twentieth Century
New Testament

But immediately, a woman having heard about Him, whose little daughter had an unclean spirit, having come, fell at His feet. And the woman was a Gentile, a Syrophoenician as to her race. And she kept on begging Him to cast out the demon out of her little daughter.

And He was saying to her, Let first the children be fed, for it is not right to take the bread of the children and to throw it to the little pet dogs.

But she answered and says to Him, Yes, Sir, yet the little pet dogs under the table are constantly eating from the little morsels of the little children.

And He said to her, Because of this word, be going; the demon is gone out of your daughter.

And having gone off into her home, she found the little child lying quietly

upon her couch and the demon gone out.
Mark 7:25-30
The Wuest New Testament

And again, having gone out of the region of Tyre, He went through Sidon to the sea of Galilee in the midst of the region of Decapolis. And they bring to Him one who was deaf and who spoke with difficulty.

And they beg Him to place upon him His hand. And having taken him away from the crowd, in private He put His fingers into his ears, and having spit, He touched his tongue.

And having looked up into heaven, He groaned and says to him, Ephphatha, which is, Be opened. And his ears opened, and immediately that which bound his tongue was loosed, and he began to be enunciating correctly.

Mark 7:31-35
The Wuest New Testament

So they arrived at Bethsaida where a blind man was brought to him, with the earnest request that he should touch him.

Jesus took the blind man's hand and led him outside the village. Then he moistened his eyes with saliva and putting his hands on him, asked, "Can you see at all?"

The man looked up and said, "I can see people. They look like trees — only they are walking about."

Then Jesus put his hands on his eyes once more and his sight came into focus, and he recovered and saw everything sharp and clear.

Mark 8:22-25
J. B. Phillips Trans.

Then one of the crowd answered and said, "Teacher, I brought You my son, who has a mute spirit.

"And wherever it seizes him, it throws him down; he foams at the mouth, gnashes his teeth, and becomes rigid. So I spoke to Your disciples, that they should cast it out, but they could not."

He answered him and said, "O faithless generation, how long shall I be with you? How long shall I bear with you? Bring him to Me."

Then they brought him to Him. And

when he saw Him, immediately the spirit convulsed him, and he fell on the ground and wallowed, foaming at the mouth.

So He asked his father, "How long has this been happening to him?" And he said, "From childhood.

"And often he has thrown him both into the fire and into the water to destroy him. But if You can do anything, have compassion on us and help us."

Jesus said to him, "If you can believe, all things are possible to him who believes."

Immediately the father of the child cried out and said with tears, "Lord, I believe; help my unbelief!"

When Jesus saw that the people came running together, He rebuked the unclean spirit, saying to it: "Deaf and dumb spirit, I command you, come out of him and enter him no more!"

Then the spirit cried out, convulsed him greatly, and came out of him. And he became as one dead, so that many said, "He is dead."

But Jesus took him by the hand and lifted him up, and he arose.

And when He had come into the house, His disciples asked Him privately, "Why could we not cast it out?"

So He said to them, "This kind can come out by nothing but prayer and fasting."

Mark 9:17-29 NKJV

And they come to Jericho: and, as He was going forth from Jericho, with His disciples and a great multitude, the son of Timaeus, Bartimaeus, a blind beggar, was sitting by the road.

And, hearing that it was Jesus the Nazarene, he began to cry out, and say, "Son of David! Jesus! have mercy on me!"

And many were rebuking him, that he should be silent. But he kept crying much more, "Son of David! have mercy on me!"

And, standing still, Jesus said, "Call him." And they call the blind man, saying to him, "Be of good cheer; arise! He is calling you!"

And he, casting away his garment, springing up, came to Jesus.

And Jesus, answering him, said, "What

do you wish that I should do for you?" And the blind man said to Him, "Rabboni, that I may receive my sight."

And Jesus said to him, "Go your way, your faith has healed you." And straightway he received sight, and was following Jesus in the way.

Mark 10:46-52

The Worrell New Testament

"Have faith in God!" replied Jesus. "I tell you that if any one should say to this hill, 'Be lifted up and hurled into the sea!' without ever a doubt in his mind, but in the faith that what he says will be done, he would find that it would be.

"And therefore I say to you, 'Have faith that whatever you ask for in prayer is already granted you, and you will find that it will be.'

"And, whenever you stand up to pray, forgive any grievance that you have against any one, that your Father who is in Heaven also may forgive you your offences."

Mark 11:22-25

The Twentieth Century
New Testament

And Jesus, replying, said to them, Have faith in God [constantly].

Truly I tell you, whoever says to this mountain, Be lifted up and thrown into the sea! and does not doubt at all in his heart but believes that what he says will take place, it will be done for him.

For this reason I am telling you, whatever you ask for in prayer, believe (trust and be confident) that it is granted to you, and you will [get it].

And whenever you stand praying, if you have anything against anyone, forgive him and let it drop (leave it, let it go), in order that your Father Who is in heaven may also forgive you your [own] failings and shortcomings and let them drop.

But if you do not forgive, neither will your Father in heaven forgive your failings and shortcomings.

Mark 11:22-26 AMP

And He said to them, "Going into all the world, preach the Gospel to the whole creation.

"He that believes and is immersed

shall be saved; but he that disbelieves shall be condemned.

"And these signs shall accompany those having believed: in My name will they cast out demons; they will speak with tongues;

"They will take up serpents; and, if they drink any deadly thing, it will not hurt them; they will lay hands on the sick, and they will recover."

The Lord Jesus, therefore, after He spake to them, was caught up into Heaven, and sat down at the right hand of God.

And they, going forth, preached everywhere, the Lord working with them, and confirming the word through the signs closely following.

Mark 16:15-20
The Worrell New Testament

For with God nothing shall be impossible.

Luke 1:37

For no promise of God can fail to be fulfilled.

Luke 1:37
J. B. Phillips Trans.

And he came to Nazareth, where he had been brought up: and, as his custom was, he went into the synagogue on the sabbath day, and stood up for to read.

And there was delivered unto him the book of the prophet Esaias. And when he had opened the book, he found the place where it was written,

The Spirit of the Lord is upon me, because he hath anointed me to preach the gospel to the poor; he hath sent me to heal the brokenhearted, to preach deliverance to the captives, and recovering of sight to the blind, to set at liberty them that are bruised,

To preach the acceptable year of the Lord.

And he closed the book, and he gave it again to the minister, and sat down. And the eyes of all them that were in the synagogue were fastened on him.

And he began to say unto them, This day is this scripture fulfilled in your ears.

Luke 4:16-21

And having arisen from the teacher's chair in the synagogue, He went into the home of Simon. Now, the mother-in-law of Simon had been afflicted for some time with a chronic fever, a severe one. And they made request of Him in her behalf. And having taken His stand over her, He rebuked the fever, and it left her. And instantly, having stood up, she served food and drink to them.

Luke 4:38,39
The Wuest New Testament

Now when the sun was setting, all they that had any sick with divers diseases brought them unto him; and he laid his hands on every one of them, and healed them.

Luke 4:40

Then, as the sun was setting, all those who had friends suffering from every kind of disease brought them to Jesus and he laid his hands on each one of them separately and healed them. Evil spirits came out of many of these people, shouting, "You are the Son of God!"

Luke 4:40,41
J. B. Phillips Trans.

67

And it came to pass, when he was in a certain city, behold a man full of leprosy: who seeing Jesus fell on his face, and besought him, saying, Lord, if thou wilt, thou canst make me clean.

And he put forth his hand, and touched him, saying, I will: be thou clean. And immediately the leprosy departed from him.

And he charged him to tell no man: but go, and shew thyself to the priest, and offer for thy cleansing, according as Moses commanded, for a testimony unto them.

But so much the more went there a fame abroad of him: and great multitudes came together to hear, and to be healed by him of their infirmities.

Luke 5:12-15

On one occasion Jesus was staying in a town, when he saw a man who was covered with leprosy. When the leper saw Jesus, he threw himself on his face and implored his help: "Master, if only you are willing, you are able to make me clean."

Stretching out his hand, Jesus touched him, saying as he did so: "I am willing;

become clean."

Instantly the leprosy left the man; and then Jesus impressed upon him that he was not to say a word to any one, "but," he added, "set out and show yourself to the Priest, and make the offerings for your cleansing, in the manner directed by Moses, as evidence of your cure."

However, the story about Jesus spread all the more, and great crowds came together to listen to him, and to be cured of their illnesses.

Luke 5:12-15
The Twentieth Century
New Testament

One day while Jesus was teaching, some Pharisees and experts in the Law were sitting near him. They had come out of every village in Galilee and Judaea as well as from Jerusalem.

The Lord's power to heal people was with him. Soon some men arrived carrying a paralytic on a small bed and they kept trying to carry him in to put him down in front of Jesus.

When they failed to find a way of getting him in because of the dense crowd, they went up on to the top of the house and let him down, bed and all, through the tiles, into the middle of the crowd in front of Jesus. When Jesus saw their faith, he said to the man, "My friend, your sins are forgiven."

The scribes and the Pharisees began to argue about this, saying, "Who is this man who talks blasphemy? Who can forgive sins? Only God can do that."

Jesus realised what was going on in their minds and spoke straight to them.

"Why must you argue like this in your minds? Which do you suppose is easier — to say, 'Your sins are forgiven' or to say, 'Get up and walk'? But to make you realise that the Son of Man has full authority on earth to forgive sins — I tell you," he said to the man who was paralysed, "get up, pick up your bed and go home!"

Instantly the man sprang to his feet before their eyes, picked up the bedding on which he used to lie, and went off home, praising God.

Sheer amazement gripped every man present, and they praised God and said in

awed voices, "We have seen incredible
things today."

Luke 5:17-26
J. B. Phillips Trans.

One day as he was teaching, and near him
sat Pharisees and doctors of the Law who
had come from every village of Galilee and
Judaea as well as from Jerusalem. Now the
power of the Lord was present for the work
of healing.

Some men came up, carrying a man
who was paralysed; they tried to carry him
inside and lay him in front of Jesus, but
when they could not find any means of
getting him in, on account of the crowd,
they climbed to the top of the house and
let him down through the tiles, mattress
and all, among people in front of Jesus.

When he saw their faith, he said,
"Man, your sins are forgiven you."

Then the scribes and Pharisees began
to argue, "Who is this blasphemer? Who
can forgive sins, who but God alone?"

Conscious that they were arguing to
themselves, Jesus addressed them, saying,
"Why argue in your hearts? Which is the

easier thing, to say, 'Your sins are forgiven,'
or to say, 'Rise and walk'? But to let you see
the Son of man has power on earth to forgive sins" — he said to the paralysed man,
"Rise, I tell you, lift your mattress and go
home."

Instantly he got up before them, lifted
what he had been lying on, and went
home glorifying God.

And all were seized with astonishment; they glorified God and were filled
with awe, saying, "We have seen incredible
things today."

Luke 5:17-26
Moffatt's Trans.

And it came to pass also on another sabbath, that he entered into the synagogue
and taught: and there was a man whose
right hand was withered.

And the scribes and Pharisees
watched him, whether he would heal on
the sabbath day; that they might find an
accusation against him.

But he knew their thoughts, and said
to the man which had the withered hand,
Rise up, and stand forth in the midst. And

he arose and stood forth.

Then said Jesus unto them, I will ask you one thing; Is it lawful on the sabbath days to do good, or to do evil? to save life, or to destroy it?

And looking round about upon them all, he said unto the man, Stretch forth thy hand. And he did so: and his hand was restored whole as the other.

Luke 6:6-10

And he came down with them, and stood in the plain, and the company of his disciples, and a great multitude of people out of all Judaea and Jerusalem, and from the sea coast of Tyre and Sidon, which came to hear him, and to be healed of their diseases;

And they that were vexed with unclean spirits: and they were healed.

And the whole multitude sought to touch him: for there went virtue out of him, and healed them all.

Luke 6:17-19

He went down with them and stood on a

level place. A large crowd of his disciples was there and a great number of people from all over Judea, from Jerusalem, and from the coast of Tyre and Sidon,

Who had come to hear him and to be healed of their diseases. Those troubled by evil spirits were cured,

And the people all tried to touch him, because power was coming from him and healing them all.

Luke 6:17-19 NIV

Now when he had ended all his sayings in the audience of the people, he entered into Capernaum.

And a certain centurion's servant, who was dear unto him, was sick, and ready to die.

And when he heard of Jesus, he sent unto him the elders of the Jews, beseeching him that he would come and heal his servant.

And when they came to Jesus, they besought him instantly, saying, That he was worthy for whom he should do this:

For he loveth our nation, and he hath built us a synagogue.

Then Jesus went with them. And when he was now not far from the house, the centurion sent friends to him, saying unto him, Lord, trouble not thyself: for I am not worthy that thou shouldest enter under my roof:

Wherefore neither thought I myself worthy to come unto thee: but say in a word, and my servant shall be healed.

For I also am a man set under authority, having under me soldiers, and I say unto one, Go, and he goeth; and to another, Come, and he cometh; and to my servant, Do this, and he doeth it.

When Jesus heard these things, he marvelled at him, and turned him about, and said unto the people that followed him, I say unto you, I have not found so great faith, no, not in Israel.

And they that were sent, returning to the house, found the servant whole that had been sick.

Luke 7:1-10

And it came to pass the day after, that he went into a city called Nain; and many of his disciples went with him, and much people.

Now when he came nigh to the gate of the city, behold, there was a dead man carried out, the only son of his mother, and she was a widow: and much people of the city was with her.

And when the Lord saw her, he had compassion on her, and said unto her, Weep not.

And he came and touched the bier: and they that bare him stood still. And he said, Young man, I say unto thee, Arise.

And he that was dead sat up, and began to speak. And he delivered him to his mother.

Luke 7:11-15

When the men were come unto him, they said, John Baptist hath sent us unto thee, saying, Art thou he that should come? or look we for another?

And in that same hour he cured many of their infirmities and plagues, and of evil spirits; and unto many that were blind he gave sight.

Then Jesus answering said unto them, Go your way, and tell John what things ye have seen and heard; how that the blind see, the lame walk, the lepers are cleansed, the deaf hear, the dead are raised, to the poor the gospel is preached.

And blessed is he, whosoever shall not be offended in me.

Luke 7:20-23

As they went a woman who wanted to be healed came up behind and touched him, for she had been slowly bleeding for twelve years, and could find no cure (though she had spent everything she had on doctors). But the instant she touched the edge of his robe, the bleeding stopped.

"Who touched me?" Jesus asked.

Everyone denied it, and Peter said, "Master, so many are crowding against you...."

But Jesus told him, "No, it was someone *who deliberately touched me*, for I felt healing power go out from me."

When the woman realized that Jesus knew, she began to tremble and fell to her knees before him and told why she had touched him and that now she was well.

"Daughter," he said to her, "your faith has healed you. Go in peace."

Luke 8:43-48 TLB

While he was still speaking to her, a messenger arrived from the Jairus' home with the news that the little girl was dead. "She's gone," he told her father; "there's no use troubling the Teacher now."

But when Jesus heard what had happened, he said to the father, "Don't be afraid! Just trust me, and she'll be all right."

When they arrived at the house Jesus wouldn't let anyone into the room except Peter, James, John, and the little girl's father and mother.

The home was filled with mourning people, but he said, "Stop the weeping! She isn't dead; she is only asleep!" This brought scoffing and laughter, for they all knew she was dead.

Then he took her by the hand and called, "Get up, little girl!" And at that moment her life returned and she jumped up! "Give her something to eat!" he said. Her parents were overcome with happiness, but Jesus insisted that they not tell anyone the details of what had happened.

Luke 8:49-56 TLB

Then he called his twelve disciples together, and gave them power and authority over all devils, and to cure diseases.

And he sent them to preach the kingdom of God, and to heal the sick.

And they departed, and went through the towns, preaching the gospel, and healing every where.

Luke 9:1,2,6

And the people, when they knew it, followed him: and he received them, and spake unto them of the kingdom of God, and healed them that had need of healing.

Luke 9:11

Next day, when they came down the hill, a large crowd met him. "Teacher," shouted a man from the crowd, "look at my son, I beg of you, for he is my only boy, and a spirit gets hold of him till he suddenly shrieks; it convulses him till he foams; indeed it will hardly leave off tearing him to pieces. I begged your disciples to cast it out, but they could not."

Jesus answered, "O faithless and perverse generation, how long must I still be with you and bear with you? Fetch your son here."

Before the boy could reach Jesus, the demon dashed him down and convulsed him; but Jesus checked the unclean spirit, cured the boy, and handed him back to his father.

All were astounded at this grand display of God.

Luke 9:37-43
Moffatt's Trans.

Behold, I give unto you power to tread on serpents and scorpions, and over all the power of the enemy: and nothing shall by any means hurt you.
Luke 10:19

I have indeed given you the power of treading on serpents and scorpions and of trampling down all the power of the Enemy; nothing shall injure you.
Luke 10:19
Moffatt's Trans.

A woman had a spirit that caused an infirmity eighteen years and was completely bent together by a curvature of the spine, and was not able to raise herself up at all. And having seen her, Jesus called her and said to her, Woman, you have been released from your infirmity, and the cure is permanent.

And He placed His hands on her. And immediately she was restored to an erect position. And she glorified God.

But the ruler of the synagogue answering, being indignant that on the sabbath Jesus had healed, was saying to the crowd, Six days there are during which it is right and proper to accomplish things. In them therefore you should come and be healed, and not on the day of the sabbath. But the Lord answered him and said, Actors on the stage of life, playing the role of that which you are not, does not each one of you on the sabbath release his ox or his donkey from the feeding-trough and lead it off to give it a drink?

And this woman, being a daughter of Abraham, whom Satan bound, just think of it, eighteen years, was it not a necessity in the nature of the case that she be released from this binding restriction on the sabbath?

And while He was saying these things, all those who had opposed Him blushed for shame. And the entire crowd went to rejoicing because of all the glorious things which were being done by Him.

Luke 13:11-17
The Wuest New Testament

And it came to pass, as he went into the house of one of the chief Pharisees to eat bread on the sabbath day, that they watched him.

And, behold, there was a certain man before him which had the dropsy.

And Jesus answering spake unto the lawyers and Pharisees, saying, Is it lawful to heal on the sabbath day?

And they held their peace. And he [Jesus] took him, and healed him, and let him go.

Luke 14:1-4

And it came to pass, as he went to Jerusalem, that he passed through the midst of Samaria and Galilee.

And as he entered into a certain village, there met him ten men that were lepers, which stood afar off:

And they lifted up their voices, and said, Jesus, Master, have mercy on us.

And when he saw them, he said unto them, Go shew yourselves unto the priests. And it came to pass, that, as they went, they were cleansed.

And one of them, when he saw that he was healed, turned back, and with a loud voice glorified God,

And fell down on his face at his feet, giving him thanks: and he was a Samaritan.

And Jesus answering said, Were there not ten cleansed? but where are the nine?

There are not found that returned to give glory to God, save this stranger.

And he said unto him, Arise, go thy way: thy faith hath made thee whole.

Luke 17:11-19

And it came to pass, when He was drawing near to Jericho, that a certain blind man was sitting by the wayside, begging.

And, hearing a multitude passing along, he was inquiring what this might be.

And they told him, that Jesus the

Nazarene was passing by.

And he cried, saying, "Jesus, Son of David, have mercy on me!"

And those going before were rebuking him, that he should be silent; but he kept crying out much more, "Son of David, have mercy on me!"

And Jesus, standing still, commanded that he be brought to Him; and, when he drew near, He asked him,

"What do you wish that I should do for you?" And he said, "Lord, that I may receive sight."

And Jesus said to him, "Receive sight; your faith has made you whole."

And instantly he received sight, and was following Him, glorifying God. And all the people, seeing it, gave praise to God.

Luke 18:35-43

The Worrell New Testament

Now when the supporters of Jesus saw what was going to happen, they said, "Lord, shall we strike with our swords?"

One of them did strike the servant of the high priest, cutting off his right ear;

But Jesus said, "No more of that!" and

cured him by touching his ear.

Luke 22:49-51

Moffatt's Trans.

So Jesus came again to Cana of Galilee where He had made the water wine. And there was a certain nobleman whose son was sick at Capernaum.

When he heard that Jesus had come out of Judea into Galilee, he went to Him and implored Him to come down and heal his son, for he was at the point of death.

Then Jesus said to him, "Unless you people see signs and wonders, you will by no means believe."

The nobleman said to Him, "Sir, come down before my child dies!"

Jesus said to him, "Go your way; your son lives." So the man believed the word that Jesus spoke to him, and he went his way.

And as he was now going down, his servants met him and told him, saying, "Your son lives!"

Then he inquired of them the hour when he got better. And they said to him, "Yesterday at the seventh hour the fever left him."

So the father knew that it was at the same hour in which Jesus said to him, "Your son lives." And he himself believed, and his whole household.

John 4:46-53 NKJV

After this there was a feast of the Jews; and Jesus went up to Jerusalem.

Now there is at Jerusalem by the sheep market a pool, which is called in the Hebrew tongue Bethesda, having five porches.

In these lay a great multitude of impotent folk, of blind, halt, withered, waiting for the moving of the water.

For an angel went down at a certain season into the pool, and troubled the water: whosoever then first after the troubling of the water stepped in was made whole of whatsoever disease he had.

And a certain man was there, which had an infirmity thirty and eight years.

When Jesus saw him lie, and knew that he had been now a long time in that case, he saith unto him, Wilt thou be made whole?

The impotent man answered him, Sir,

I have no man, when the water is troubled, to put me into the pool: but while I am coming, another steppeth down before me.

Jesus saith unto him, Rise, take up thy bed, and walk.

And immediately the man was made whole, and took up his bed, and walked.
John 5:1-9

It is the spirit that quickeneth; the flesh profiteth nothing: the words that I speak unto you, they are spirit, and they are life.
John 6:63

And as Jesus passed by, he saw a man which was blind from his birth.

And his disciples asked him, saying, Master, who did sin, this man, or his parents, that he was born blind?

Jesus answered, Neither hath this man sinned, nor his parents: but that the works of God should be made manifest in him.

I must work the works of him that sent me, while it is day: the night cometh, when no man can work.

As long as I am in the world, I am the light of the world.

When he had thus spoken, he spat on the ground, and made clay of the spittle, and he anointed the eyes of the blind man with the clay,

And said unto him, Go, wash in the pool of Siloam, (which is by interpretation, Sent.) He went his way therefore, and washed, and came seeing.

The neighbours therefore, and they which before had seen him that he was blind, said, Is not this he that sat and begged?

Some said, This is he: others said, He is like him: but he said, I am he.

Therefore said they unto him, How were thine eyes opened?

He answered and said, A man is called Jesus made clay, and anointed mine eyes, and said unto me, Go to the pool of Siloam, and wash: and I went and washed, and I received sight.

John 9:1-11

The thief [Satan] comes only in order to steal and kill and destroy. I came that they may have and enjoy life, and have it in abundance (to the full, till it overflows).

John 10:10 AMP

The thief does not come except to steal and to kill and to destroy. I alone came in order that they might be possessing life, and that they might be possessing it in superabundance.

John 10:10
The Wuest New Testament

Now a man named Lazarus was sick. He was from Bethany, the village of Mary and her sister Martha. This Mary, whose brother Lazarus now lay sick, was the same one who poured perfume on the Lord and wiped his feet with her hair. So the sisters sent word to Jesus, "Lord, the one you love is sick."

When he heard this, Jesus said, "This sickness will not end in death. No, it is for God's glory so that God's Son may be glorified through it." Jesus loved Martha and her sister and Lazarus. Yet when he heard that Lazarus was sick, he stayed where he was two more days.

Then he said to his disciples, "Let us go back to Judea."

"But Rabbi," they said, "a short while ago the Jews tried to stone you, and yet you are going back there?"

Jesus answered, "Are there not twelve hours of daylight? A man who walks by day will not stumble, for he sees by this world's light. It is when he walks by night that he stumbles, for he has no light."

After he had said this, he went on to tell them, "Our friend Lazarus has fallen asleep; but I am going there to wake him up."

His disciples replied, "Lord, if he sleeps, he will get better." Jesus had been speaking of his death, but his disciples thought he meant natural sleep.

So then he told them plainly, "Lazarus is dead, and for your sake I am glad I was not there, so that you may believe. But let us go to him."

Then Thomas (called Didymus) said to the rest of the disciples, "Let us also go, that we may die with him."

On his arrival, Jesus found that Lazarus had already been in the tomb for four days. Bethany was less than two miles from Jerusalem, and many Jews had come to Martha and Mary to comfort them in the loss of their brother. When Martha heard that Jesus was coming, she went out to meet him, but Mary stayed at home.

"Lord," Martha said to Jesus, "if you had been here, my brother would not have died. But I know that even now God will give you whatever you ask."

Jesus said to her, "Your brother will rise again."

Martha answered, "I know he will rise again in the resurrection at the last day."

Jesus said to her, "I am the resurrection and the life. He who believes in me will live, even though he dies; and whoever lives and believes in me will never die. Do you believe this?"

"Yes, Lord," she told him, "I believe that you are the Christ, the Son of God, who was to come into the world."

And after she had said this, she went back and called her sister Mary aside. "The Teacher is here," she said, "and is asking for you." When Mary heard this, she got up quickly and went to him. Now Jesus had not yet entered the village, but was still at the place where Martha had met him.

When the Jews who had been with Mary in the house, comforting her, noticed how quickly she got up and went out, they followed her, supposing she was going to the tomb to mourn there.

When Mary reached the place where Jesus was and saw him, she fell at his feet and said, "Lord, if you had been here, my brother would not have died."

When Jesus saw her weeping, and the Jews who had come along with her also weeping, he was deeply moved in spirit and troubled. "Where have you laid him?" he asked.

"Come and see, Lord," they replied.

Jesus wept.

Then the Jews said, "See how he loved him!"

But some of them said, "Could not he who opened the eyes of the blind man have kept this man from dying?"

Jesus, once more deeply moved, came to the tomb. It was a cave with a stone laid across the entrance. "Take away the stone," he said.

"But, Lord," said Martha, the sister of the dead man, "by this time there is a bad odor, for he has been there four days."

Then Jesus said, "Did I not tell you that if you believed, you would see the glory of God?"

So they took away the stone. Then Jesus looked up and said, "Father, I thank you that you have heard me. I knew that you always hear me, but I said this for the benefit of the people standing here, that they may believe that you sent me."

When he had said this, Jesus called in a loud voice, "Lazarus, come out!" The dead man came out, his hands and feet wrapped with strips of linen, and a cloth around his face.

Jesus said to them, "Take off the grave clothes and let him go."

John 11:1-44 NIV

And whatsoever ye shall ask in my name, that will I do, that the Father may be glorified in the Son.

If ye shall ask any thing in my name, I will do it.

John 14:13,14

I am the real Vine, and my Father is the

vinedresser; he cuts away any branch on me which is not bearing fruit, and cleans every branch which does bear fruit, to make it bear richer fruit.

You are already clean, by the word I have spoken to you. Remain in me, as I remain in you: just as a branch cannot bear fruit by itself, without remaining on the vine, neither can you, unless you remain in me.

I am the vine, you are the branches. He who remains in me, as I in him, bears rich fruit (because apart from me you can do nothing).

If anyone does not remain in me, he is thrown aside like a branch and he withers up; then the branches are gathered and thrown into the fire to be burned.

If you remain in me and my words remain in you, then ask whatever you like and you shall have it.

John 15:1-7
Moffatt's Trans.

I assure you, most solemnly I tell you, that My Father will grant you whatever you ask in My Name [as presenting all that I AM].

Up to this time you have not asked a [single] thing in My Name [as presenting all that I AM]; but now ask and keep on asking and you will receive, so that your joy (gladness, delight) may be full and complete.

John 16:23,24 AMP

Now Peter and John went up together into the temple at the hour of prayer, being the ninth hour.

And a certain man lame from his mother's womb was carried, whom they laid daily at the gate of the temple which is called Beautiful, to ask alms of them that entered into the temple;

Who seeing Peter and John about to go into the temple asked an alms.

And Peter, fastening his eyes upon him with John, said, Look on us.

And he gave heed unto them, expecting to receive something of them.

Then Peter said, Silver and gold have I none; but such as I have give I thee: In the name of Jesus Christ of Nazareth rise up and walk.

And he took him by the right hand,

and lifted him up: and immediately his feet and ankle bones received strength.

And he leaping up stood, and walked, and entered with them into the temple, walking, and leaping, and praising God.

And his name [Jesus' name] through faith in his name hath made this man strong, whom ye see and know: yea, the faith which is by him hath given him this perfect soundness in the presence of you all.

Acts 3:1-8,16

Then Peter, filled with the Holy Ghost, said unto them, Ye rulers of the people, and elders of Israel,

If we this day be examined of the good deed done to the impotent man, by what means he is made whole;

Be it known unto you all, and to all the people of Israel, that by the name of Jesus Christ of Nazareth, whom ye crucified, whom God raised from the dead, even by him doth this man stand here before you whole.

Acts 4:8-10

And being let go, they [Peter and John] went to their own company, and reported all that the chief priests and elders had said unto them.

And when they heard that, they lifted up their voice to God with one accord, and said, Lord, thou art God, which hast made heaven, and earth, and the sea, and all that in them is:

Who by the mouth of thy servant David hast said, Why did the heathen rage, and the people imagine vain things?

The kings of the earth stood up, and the rulers were gathered together against the Lord, and against his Christ.

For of a truth against thy holy child Jesus, whom thou hast anointed, both Herod, and Pontius Pilate, with the Gentiles, and the people of Israel, were gathered together,

For to do whatsoever thy hand and thy counsel determined before to be done.

And now, Lord, behold their threatenings: and grant unto thy servants, that with all boldness they may speak thy word,

By stretching forth thine hand to heal;

and that signs and wonders may be done by the name of thy holy child Jesus.

And when they had prayed, the place was shaken where they were assembled together; and they were all filled with the Holy Ghost, and they spake the word of God with boldness.

Acts 4:23-31

And by the hands of the apostles were many signs and wonders wrought among the people; (and they were all with one accord in Solomon's porch.

And of the rest durst no man join himself to them: but the people magnified them.

And believers were the more added to the Lord, multitudes both of men and women.)

Insomuch that they brought forth the sick into the streets, and laid them on beds and couches, that at the least the shadow of Peter passing by might overshadow some of them.

There came also a multitude out of the cities round about unto Jerusalem, bringing sick folks, and them which were vexed with unclean spirits: and they were healed every one.

Acts 5:12-16

And Stephen, full of faith and power, did great wonders and miracles among the people.

Acts 6:8

Then Philip went down to the city of Samaria, and preached Christ unto them.

And the people with one accord gave heed unto those things which Philip spake, hearing and seeing the miracles which he did.

For unclean spirits, crying with loud voice, came out of many that were possessed with them: and many taken with palsies, and that were lame, were healed.

And there was great joy in that city.

Acts 8:5-8

Now it happened that Peter, in the course of travelling about among them all, came down to God's people living at Lydda.

There he found a man called Aeneas who had been bed-ridden for eight years through paralysis. Peter said to him, "Aeneas, Jesus Christ heals you! Get up and make your bed."

He got to his feet at once. And all those who lived in Lydda and Sharon saw him and turned to the Lord.

Acts 9:32-35

J. B. Phillips Trans.

How God anointed Jesus of Nazareth with the Holy Ghost and with power: who went about doing good, and healing all that were oppressed of the devil; for God was with him.

Acts 10:38

And there sat a certain man at Lystra, impotent in his feet, being a cripple from his mother's womb, who never had walked:

The same heard Paul speak: who stedfastly beholding him, and perceiving that he had faith to be healed,

Said with a loud voice, Stand upright

on thy feet. And he leaped and walked.
Acts 14:8-10

And God did unusual and extraordinary miracles by the hands of Paul,

So that handkerchiefs or towels or aprons which had touched his skin were carried away and put upon the sick, and their diseases left them and the evil spirits came out of them.
Acts 19:11,12 AMP

And it came to pass, that the father of Publius lay sick of a fever and of a bloody flux: to whom Paul entered in, and prayed, and laid his hands on him, and healed him.

So when this was done, others also, which had diseases in the island, came, and were healed.
Acts 28:8,9

(As it is written, I have made thee a father of many nations,) before him whom he believed, even God, who quickeneth the dead, and calleth those things which be not as though they were.

Who against hope believed in hope, that he might become the father of many nations, according to that which was spoken, So shall thy seed be.

And being not weak in faith, he [Abraham] considered not his own body now dead, when he was about an hundred years old, neither yet the deadness of Sarah's womb:

He staggered not at the promise of God through unbelief; but was strong in faith, giving glory to God;

And being fully persuaded that, what he had promised, he was able also to perform.

Romans 4:17-21

But if the Spirit of him that raised up Jesus from the dead dwell in you, he that raised up Christ from the dead shall also quicken your mortal bodies by his Spirit that dwelleth in you.

Therefore, brethren, we are debtors, not to the flesh, to live after the flesh.

For if ye live after the flesh, ye shall die: but if ye through the Spirit do mortify the deeds of the body, ye shall live.

Romans 8:11-13

Likewise the Spirit also helpeth our infirmities: for we know not what we should pray for as we ought: but the Spirit itself [Himself] maketh intercession for us with groanings which cannot be uttered.

And he that searcheth the hearts knoweth what is the mind of the Spirit, because he maketh intercession for the saints according to the will of God.

Romans 8:26,27

For I have received of the Lord that which also I delivered unto you, That the Lord Jesus the same night in which he was betrayed took bread:

And when he had given thanks, he brake it, and said, Take, eat: this is my body, which is broken for you: this do in remembrance of me.

After the same manner also he took the cup, when he had supped, saying, This cup is the new testament in my blood: this do ye, as oft as ye drink it, in remembrance of me.

For as often as ye eat this bread, and drink this cup, ye do shew the Lord's death till he come.

Wherefore whosoever shall eat this bread, and drink this cup of the Lord, unworthily, shall be guilty of the body and blood of the Lord.

But let a man examine himself, and so let him eat of that bread, and drink of that cup.

For he that eateth and drinketh unworthily, eateth and drinketh damnation to himself, not discerning the Lord's body.

For this cause many are weak and sickly among you, and many sleep.

For if we would judge ourselves, we should not be judged.

1 Corinthians 11:23-31

Now concerning the spiritual gifts, brethren, I do not wish you to be ignorant.

Ye know that ye were gentiles, carried

away to the dumb idols, as ye were led.

Wherefore, I make known to you that no one speaking in the Spirit of God, says, "Jesus is accursed"; and no one can say, "Jesus is Lord," except in the Holy Spirit.

Now there are diversities of gifts, but the same Spirit.

And there are diversities of ministries, and the same Lord.

And there are diversities of workings, but the same God, Who worketh all things in all.

And to each one is given the manifestation of the Spirit for profiting.

For to one, indeed, is given through the Spirit a word of wisdom; and to another, a word of knowledge, according to the same Spirit;

To another, faith, in the same Spirit; and to another, *gifts of healings*, in the one Spirit;

And to another, workings of mighty deeds; and to another, prophecy; and to another, discerning of spirits; to another, various kinds of tongues; and to another, interpretation of tongues.

But all these worketh the one and the same Spirit, distributing to each one, severally, even as He willeth.

1 Corinthians 12:1-11
The Worrell New Testament

And God, indeed, set some in the assembly: first, apostles; second, prophets; third, teachers; after that, miracles; then, *gifts of healings,* helps, governments, various kinds of tongues.

Are all apostles? Are all prophets? Are all teachers? Are all workers of miracles?

Do all have gifts of healings? Do all speak with tongues? Do all interpret?

But desire earnestly the greater gifts; and a still more excellent way I show you.

1 Corinthians 12:28-31
The Worrell New Testament

For though we walk in the flesh, we do not war after the flesh:

(For the weapons of our warfare are not carnal, but mighty through God to the pulling down of strong holds;)

Casting down imaginations, and every high thing that exalteth itself against the knowledge of God, and bringing into captivity every thought to the obedience of Christ.

2 Corinthians 10:3-5

For though we live in the world, we do not wage war as the world does.

The weapons we fight with are not the weapons of the world. On the contrary, they have divine power to demolish strongholds.

We demolish arguments and every pretension that sets itself up against the knowledge of God, and we take captive every thought to make it obedient to Christ

2 Corinthians 10:3-5 NIV

Christ hath redeemed us from the curse of the law, being made a curse for us: for it is written, Cursed is every one that hangeth on a tree:

That the blessing of Abraham might come on the Gentiles through Jesus Christ; that we might receive the promise of the Spirit through faith.

And if ye be Christ's, then are ye Abraham's seed, and heirs according to the promise.

Galatians 3:13,14,29

Let all bitterness, and wrath, and anger, and clamour, and evil speaking, be put away from you, with all malice:

And be ye kind one to another, tenderhearted, forgiving one another, even as God for Christ's sake hath forgiven you.

Ephesians 4:31,32

Children, obey your parents, as children of the Lord; for that is but right.

"Honour thy father and mother" — this is the first Commandment with a promise — "so that thou mayest prosper and have a long life on earth."

Ephesians 6:1-3
The Twentieth Century
New Testament

In conclusion, be strong in the Lord [be empowered through your union with Him]; draw your strength from Him [that strength which His boundless might provides].

Put on God's whole armor [the armor of a heavy-armed soldier which God supplies], that you may be able successfully to stand up against [all] the strategies and the deceits of the devil.

For we are not wrestling with flesh and blood [contending only with physical opponents], but against the despotisms, against the powers, against [the master spirits who are] the world rulers of this present darkness, against the spirit forces of wickedness in the heavenly (supernatural) sphere.

Therefore put on God's complete armor, that you may be able to resist and stand your ground on the evil day [of danger], and, having done all [the crisis demands], to stand [firmly in your place].

Stand therefore [hold your ground], having tightened the belt of truth around your loins and having put on the breast-plate of integrity and of moral rectitude and right standing with God.

And having shod your feet in preparation [to face the enemy with the firm-footed stability, the promptness, and the readiness produced by the good news] of the Gospel of peace.

Lift up over all the [covering] shield of saving faith, upon which you can quench all the flaming missiles of the wicked [one].

And take the helmet of salvation and the sword that the Spirit wields, which is the Word of God.

Pray at all times (on every occasion, in every season) in the Spirit, with all [manner of] prayer and entreaty. To that end keep alert and watch with strong purpose and perseverance, interceding in behalf of all the saints (God's consecrated people).

Ephesians 6:10-18 AMP

Being confident of this very thing, that he

which hath begun a good work in you will perform it until the day of Jesus Christ.
Philippians 1:6

Being confident of this, that he who began a good work in you will carry it on to completion until the day of Christ Jesus.
Philippians 1:6 NIV

Let this mind be in you, which was also in Christ Jesus:

Who, being in the form of God, thought it not robbery to be equal with God:

But made himself of no reputation, and took upon him the form of a servant, and was made in the likeness of men:

And being found in fashion as a man, he humbled himself, and became obedient unto death, even the death of the cross.

Wherefore God also hath highly exalted him, and given him a name which is above every name:

That at the name of Jesus every knee

should bow, of things in heaven, and things in earth, and things under the earth;

And that every tongue should confess that Jesus Christ is Lord, to the glory of God the Father.

Philippians 2:5-11

And the very God of peace sanctify you wholly; and I pray God your whole spirit and soul and body be preserved blameless unto the coming of our Lord Jesus Christ.

1 Thessalonians 5:23

Notwithstanding she shall be saved in childbearing, if they continue in faith and charity and holiness with sobriety.

1 Timothy 2:15

Seeing then that we have a great high priest, that is passed into the heavens, Jesus the Son of God, let us hold fast our profession.

For we have not an high priest which cannot be touched with the feeling of our infirmities; but was in all points tempted like as we are, yet without sin.

Let us therefore come boldly unto the throne of grace, that we may obtain mercy, and find grace to help in time of need.

Hebrews 4:14-16

That we be not slothful, but followers of them who through faith and patience inherit the promises.

For when God made promise to Abraham, because he could swear by no greater, he sware by himself,

Saying, Surely blessing I will bless thee, and multiplying I will multiply thee.

Hebrews 6:12-14

Let us hold fast the profession of our faith without wavering; (for he is faithful that promised).

Hebrews 10:23

Let us maintain the confession of our hope unshaken, for he who has given us his promise will not fail us.

Hebrews 10:23

The Twentieth Century
New Testament

Cast not away therefore your confidence, which hath great recompence of reward.

For ye have need of patience, that, after ye have done the will of God, ye might receive the promise.

Hebrews 10:35,36

But without faith it is impossible to please him; for he that cometh to God must believe that he is, and that he is a rewarder of them that diligently seek him.

Hebrews 11:6

See to it that no one misses the grace of God, that no root of bitterness grows up to be a trouble by contaminating all the rest of you.

Hebrews 12:15

Moffatt's Trans.

Jesus Christ is the same yesterday, today, and forever.

Hebrews 13:8 NKJV

But every good endowment and every complete gift must come from above, from the Father of all lights, with whom there is never the slightest variation or shadow of inconsistency.

James 1:17
J. B. Phillips Trans.

Is anyone among you afflicted? let him pray. Is anyone cheerful? let him sing praise.

Is anyone among you sick? let him call for the elders of the assembly; and let them pray over him, having anointed him with oil in the name of the Lord;

And the prayer of faith will save the sick, and the Lord will raise him up; and, if he have committed sins, it shall be forgiven him.

Confess, therefore, your sins one to another, and pray for one another, that ye may be healed. A righteous man's in wrought supplication avails much.

James 5:13-16
The Worrell New Testament

Who his own self bare our sins in his own body on the tree, that we, being dead to sins, should live unto righteousness: by whose stripes ye were healed.
1 Peter 2:24

He personally carried the load of our sins in his own body when he died on the cross, so that we can be finished with sin and live a good life from now on. For his wounds have healed ours!
1 Peter 2:24 TLB

And He Himself bore our sins in His body on the cross, that we might die to sin and live to righteousness; for by His wounds you were healed.
1 Peter 2:24 NASB

And he "himself carried our sins" in his own body to the cross, so that we might die to our sins, and live for righteousness. "His bruising was your healing."

1 Peter 2:24
The Twentieth Century
New Testament

All of you, clothe yourselves with humility toward one another, because, "God opposes the proud but gives grace to the humble."

Humble yourselves, therefore, under God's mighty hand, that he may lift you up in due time.

Cast all your anxiety on him because he cares for you.

Be self-controlled and alert. Your enemy the devil prowls around like a roaring lion looking for someone to devour.

Resist him, standing firm in the faith, because you know that your brothers throughout the world are undergoing the same kind of sufferings.

And the God of all grace, who called you to his eternal glory in Christ, after you have suffered a little while, will himself restore you

and make you strong, firm and steadfast.

1 Peter 5:5-10 NIV

The reason the Son of God was made manifest (visible) was to undo (destroy, loosen, and dissolve) the works the devil [has done].

1 John 3:8b AMP

You are of God, little children, and have overcome them, because He who is in you is greater than he who is in the world.

1 John 4:4 NKJV

And this is the confidence with which we approach him, that whenever we ask anything that is in accordance with his will, he listens to us.

And if we realize that he listens to us

— whatever we ask — we realize that we have what we have asked from him.

1 John 5:14,15
The Twentieth Century
New Testament

I wish above all things that thou mayest prosper and be in health, even as thy soul prospereth.

3 John 2

Beloved, in all things I am praying that you will be prospering, and that you will be continually having good health just as your soul is prospering.

3 John 2
The Wuest New Testament

My prayer for you, my very dear friend, is that you may be as healthy and prosperous in every way as you are in soul.

3 John 2
J. B. Phillips Trans.

Dear friend, I pray that all may be well with you and that you may have good health — I know that all is well with your soul.

3 John 2
The Twentieth Century
New Testament

And they overcame him [the devil] by the blood of the Lamb, and by the word of their testimony.

Revelation 12:11a

References

In Canada books are available from:

Word Alive
P. O. Box 670
Niverville, Manitoba
CANADA R0A 1E0

The Harrison House Vision

Proclaiming the truth and the power
Of the Gospel of Jesus Christ
With excellence;

Challenging Christians to
Live victoriously,
Grow spiritually,
Know God intimately.